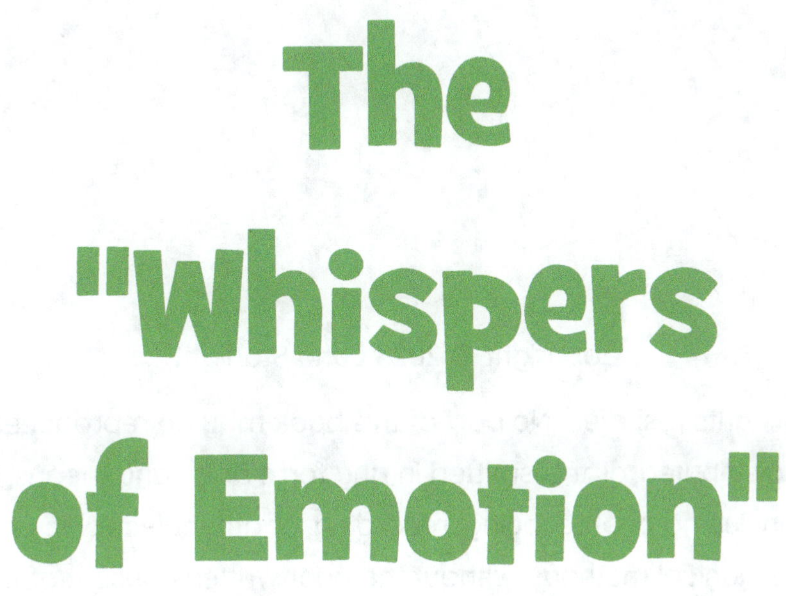

The "Whispers of Emotion"

Written by: Luna Starlight

Illustrated by: Lucinda Brush

AF390937

Copyright © 2023 Luna Starlight

All rights reserved. No part of this book may be reproduced, distributed, or transmitted in any form or by any means, including photocopying, recording, or other electronic or mechanical methods, without the prior written consent of the copyright owner, except in the case of brief quotation embodied in critical articles, reviews, and certain other noncommercial uses permitted by copyright law.

"Whispers of the World:
A Dreamer's Guide to Night-time Adventures"

"Nurture Your Bond, Spark the Imagination, and Embark on Enchanting Bedtime Adventures!"

Are you seeking an extraordinary bedtime reading experience for your child? Prepare to embark on an enchanting journey with "Whispers of the World: A Dreamer's Guide to Night-time Adventures.'" This unique series, crafted in the cosy rhythm of bedtime poems, is the perfect companion for your little one's dreamland explorations.

Explore four captivating realms - Nature, Magic, Emotion and Night-time! Each book is brimming with 15 engaging poems, designed to nurture your parent child bond, ignite your child's imagination, foster emotional understanding and soothe bedtime fears. "Whispers of the World" is more than a book series - it's a ticket to a captivating world of exploration and learning.

Imagine the delight on your child's face as they discover the whispers of nature, get thrilled by magical tales, understand their emotions more clearly and find comfort in the night's embrace. This series bridges the gap between the fascinating and the educational, leaving your child eagerly awaiting the next bedtime adventure.

Enter this journey today, take the helm and steer your child's dreams towards the captivating world of "Whispers of the World." Create memorable bedtime moments and give your child the gift of wonder, understanding and comfort that only these bedtime poems can provide.

"Whispers of Emotion"

"Exploring the Colorful Landscape of Feelings"

Prepare to guide your child gently through the intricate landscape of feelings with 'Whispers of Emotion.'

This touching book equips children with the language they need to express a rainbow of emotions - from bubbling joy to gentle sadness.

Give your child the gift of understanding their feelings and the empathy to share in the experiences of others.

Help your child navigate their emotions by adding this invaluable book to their reading list.

This Book Belongs To:

____

1. "THE SIGH OF SADNESS"

In the depths of the heart, where feelings reside,
There's a sigh of sadness that we often hide,
It whispers of rain, of tears on a rose,
Of a soft, sombre tune that ebbs and flows.

It tells of days cloudy, of the waning moon,
Of longing for melody in a lonely tune,
With a gentle exhale and a comforting pat,
Hear the whispers of sadness, in our heart's quiet chat.

2. "THE GIGGLE OF JOY"

In the peaks of delight, where happiness blooms,
There's a giggle of joy that brightens the gloom,
It bubbles with sunshine, with the chirping of lark,
With laughter that makes for a joyous spark.

It tells of rainbows, of a warm embrace,
Of the glow that joy brings to everyone's face,
With a twinkle in the eye and a cheerful ploy,
Join with the whispers of the giggle of joy.

3. "THE MURMUR OF LOVE"

In the soft, gentle spaces where affections flow,
There's a murmur of love that continues to grow,
It hums a tender song, a melody of the heart,
Of a bond so strong, it can never depart.

It tells of gentle whispers, of a mother's care,
Of friendships true and moments we share,
With a caring touch, a precious toy,
Listen to the murmur of love's sweet joy.

4. "THE SHOUT OF ANGER"

In the stormy corners, where tempers flare,

There's a shout of anger, a challenging stare,

It roars like thunder, fierce and loud,

An emotion strong, beneath a dark cloud.

It tells of the fiery sun, of the raging sea,

Of the power that brews when we disagree,

With a deep breath and a calming ploy,

Acknowledge the shout, but don't let it destroy.

5. "THE WHISPER OF HOPE"

In the heart's quiet alcove, where dreams are sown,

There's a whisper of hope, gently grown,

It rustles like leaves in a springtime breeze,

A promise of life's difficulties that will soon ease.

It speaks of dawning suns, of a future bright,

Of faith in the morning after the darkest night,

With prayers and a yearning in our hearts

Hear the whispers of hope before sadness starts!

6. "THE HUM OF CURIOSITY"

In the corners of the mind, where questions arise,
There's a hum of curiosity, where our interest lies,
It buzzes like a bee around the petals of thought,
Seeking answers to the mysteries that life has brought.

It speaks of unknown paths and of stars above,
Of the world wide wonders that we all dream of,
With an inquisitive mind and questions to ponder,
Join the hum of curiosity, part of life's true wonder.

7. "THE WHISPER OF FEAR"

In the shadowy recesses, where doubts reside,

There's a whisper of fear that we often hide,

It moves like a ghost in the deep, dark night,

Stirring up a feeling of eerie fright.

It tells of thorny paths, of the long, dark hall,

Of the fears that make us feel very small,

With courage in heart, strength we employ,

Face the whisper of fear, and make its power destroyed.

8. "THE SIGH OF RELIEF"

In the silent moments, when worries wane,

There's a sigh of relief after stresses and strain,

It sounds like the breeze after a storm has passed,

A calming sense of peace that we want to last.

It tells of tranquil seas, of the quiet dawn,

Of the sigh that comes when all worries are gone,

With a peaceful mind and life to enjoy,

Soothe yourself, oh! the sigh of relief's joy.

9. "THE ROAR OF EXCITEMENT"

In the vibrant corners, where the heart takes flight,

There's a roar of excitement, shining bright,

It sounds like a cheer, when a goal is won,

A rush of thrill, under the wonderous sun.

It speaks of adventures, of the joyous play,

Of the excitement that comes with every new day,

With a bounce in our step and spirits high,

Join the roar of excitement and reach for the sky.

10. "THE MURMUR OF CONTENTMENT"

In the quiet chambers, where satisfaction rests,
There's a murmur of contentment held in our chests,
It hums like a lullaby, at the close of the day,
A sense of fulfilment in many a way.

It speaks of warm hearths, of a good book's end,
Of the contentment that comes with a faithful friend,
With a grateful heart, in peace we lay,
Ah! the murmur of contentment at the end of the day.

11. "THE WHISPERS OF WONDER"

In the corners of the eyes, where awe resides,
There's whispers of wonder, where magic abides,
It twinkles like the stars, in the velvet night,
With each new marvel that comes into sight.

It tells of colourful rainbows, of the phoenix's flight,
Of the beauty around us that fills with delight,
With a gasp of awe, in wonder we stay,
Follow the whispers of wonder as they'll guide your way.

12. "THE ECHO OF ENVY"

In the corners of the heart, where desire burns,
There's an echo of envy, as the heart yearns,
It rumbles like the ocean, with waves so tall,
At what others have, making us feel small.

It tells of green fields, of what others hold,
Of the envious thoughts, often untold,
With a mindful pause, jealousy allay,
Hear the echo of envy, but let kindness hold sway.

IDVNGH7

13. "THE HUSH OF HUMILITY"

In the silent moments, when pride subsides,
There's a hush of humility, where truth resides,
It whispers softly, like a gentle stream,
Reminding us that we're part of a much greater theme.

It speaks of the vast sky and of the tall trees,
Of the humbleness we feel, in moments like these,
With modesty in mind and ego at bay,
Hear the hush of humility, let it light your way.

14. "THE ROAR OF RESOLVE"

In the depths of the spirit, where determination lives,
There's a roar of resolve, that continually gives,
It booms like a lion, in the heart's vast plains,
A testament to resilience, through all of life's pains.

It speaks of towering mountains, of the challenging climb,
Of the strength we find within, time after time,
With perseverance in heart and a steely gaze,
Hear the roar of resolve and set your spirit ablaze.

15. "THE WHISPER OF WISDOM"

In the quiet corners of the mind, where knowledge dwells,
There's a whisper of wisdom, in stories it tells,
It sounds like the wind, rustling through ancient scrolls,
Enlightening us and guiding our souls.

It tells of lessons learned, of the olden lore,
Of the wisdom gathered, from days of yore,
With an open mind, in knowledge we sway,
Hear the whisper of wisdom, let it light your way.

FINAL

"Dive into 'A Heart's Symphony,' a resonant poem that portrays emotions as notes in life's grand song, guiding your child through the rich tapestry of feelings, fostering their emotional literacy, and assuring them of your enduring presence "as you explore life's symphony of feelings together."

"A HEART'S SYMPHONY"

My child, each emotion is a note in life's grand song,
From a happiness melody to a sadness gong.
With every poem we share, a rhythm we adore,
A symphony of the heart, emotions we explore.

The whispers of emotion, in every rhyme and verse,
Shape the songs of our lives in this great universe.
In the quiet moments, when day becomes night,
Our heart's symphony plays in the soft starlight.

WHISPERS OF EMOTION BOOK: "FUN FACTS ABOUT EMOTIONS"

1. Everyone around the world experiences and understands basic emotions like happiness, sadness and fear.
2. Laughter and crying are both ways our bodies express emotion.
3. It's okay to feel more than one emotion at a time and it's quite normal!
4. Scientists believe the human brain can recognize and express at least 27 different categories of emotion!
5. Our heart rate can change when we experience strong emotions.
6. Positive emotions, like happiness and love, can help us to learn and remember better.
7. Our brains can remember emotional events better than regular events.
8. Even animals show signs of emotions!
9. Fear can sometimes be a good thing because it can protect us from danger.
10. People around the world can recognize a smile – it's a universal sign of happiness!

THANK YOU!

"Whispers of Emotion"

Dear empathetic explorers,

Thank you for embarking on this heartfelt journey through "Whispers of Emotion". Your courage in exploring the many hues of feelings is truly wonderful. I hope this book has equipped you with the language of emotions and empathy. Remember, it's okay to feel and sharing those feelings makes our world a kinder place.

With love and understanding,

Luna Starlight

ABOUT THE AUTHOR

"Welcome to the enchanting universe of 'Whispers of the World: A Dreamer's Guide to Night-time Adventures,' crafted by the imaginative Luna Starlight. Drawing inspiration from the mystical night sky, Luna, our storyteller, invites her young readers into a world of discovery and enchantment. Her captivating series of books is designed to transform each bedtime into a magical journey, igniting children's imaginations, nurturing curiosity, and fostering a deep bond between parent and child."

www.ingramcontent.com/pod-product-compliance
Lightning Source LLC
Chambersburg PA
CBHW081304130726

47998CB00010B/2922